# the
# Shortest
# guide to
# college
# admissions

by
## Jane S. Gabin, PhD

LYSTRA BOOKS
& Literary Services

The Shortest Guide to College Admissions
Copyright © Jane S. Gabin 2024
All rights reserved.

paperback ISBN  979-8-9877247-3-6

ebook ISBN 979-8-9877247-4-3

Library of Congress Control Number: 2024904289

Book design by Kelly Prelipp Lojk

Published by Lystra Books & Literary Services, LLC
391 Lystra Estates Drive, Chapel Hill, NC 27517
lystrabooks@gmail.com

*Dedicated to those nurturing and caring teachers and counselors who inspired us with their passion for learning.*

## ABOUT THE AUTHOR

**Jane S. Gabin** received her PhD at the University of North Carolina at Chapel Hill.

As senior assistant director of admissions at UNC, her duties included directing counselor relations and international admissions. She then moved to New York City, where she worked as a college advisor at private secondary schools, chiefly at the United Nations International School. Currently she runs her own educational advisory service in Chapel Hill, NC.

She is a member of NACAC (National Association for College Admission Counseling), SACAC (Southern Association for College Admission Counseling), and HECA (Higher Education Counselors' Association. She has conducted workshops at regional and national school admissions conferences, particularly on the subject of writing the essay.

Forget "The Rankings."

Your actual GPA
doesn't matter.

You are much more than
an SAT or ACT score.

READ ON.

# A WORD TO PARENTS & OTHER CAREGIVERS

You are reading this because you love your young people and want them to be successful in the college process. Please remember that this is their process, and not yours. They are filling out the applications and taking the exams, not you. You, in all likelihood, will be helping to pay for all this—but the work of applying should be theirs.

You need to have a frank conversation about finances by, at the latest, the sophomore year of high school. Students should know ahead of time when they will need to file for financial aid. Take a look at the Free Application for Federal Student Aid (FAFSA) to see what information is needed. You will find it on the **studentaid.gov** website. Please do not wait until after your student has been accepted to a certain school to say, "Sorry, we just can't afford it." That is unkind and unfair.

Do let your student take the lead in the search-and-apply process. If campus tours have to be arranged, they should make the reservations. If there are questions for an admissions office, let your student make the calls. Colleges have great respect for applicants who advocate for themselves.

What I am saying, in a nice way, is: please back off. Do not pressure your student to apply to colleges that are way, way beyond possibility. Please be supportive and positive about the schools your student prefers. Offer to read essays, but you will definitely not help if you write them yourself. At information sessions and college fairs, let the young people ask the questions; you can ask yours a little later. The college process is a major step towards your student's intellectual and emotional independence.

## LET GO AND WATCH.

# FOR HIGH SCHOOL STUDENTS

Why am I writing this book? After working in the admissions office at a major university and working as a college counselor at private schools and then as an independent college consultant, I have the knowledge and experience to state certain truths. I can explain and simplify the process. But I am not going to advocate for any particular college or university.

My grandparents were immigrants from Russia. My grandfather taught himself English from a pocket dictionary. My parents, both born in this country, did not speak English until they started at the local public school. They each began college but were unable to continue attending because of the Great Depression and they needed to work. Therefore, they impressed upon me from an early age that I <u>must</u> complete my college education. My parents introduced me to the world of poetry, opera, and political conversations. We always discussed everything.

Today I have a PhD in English. But more significantly, going to college opened up the world to me, and I am still learning. I met new people, students and professors, who had other experiences and made me realize how much I didn't know. I learned about vocal music, about poets of the 1930s, how political decisions affected my life, about Argentinian cinema, the history of the women's movement. Who knew if anything would relate to what I did for my career? But the information was there, percolating.

Now I want to use my extended experience in a number of educational systems to make your life a little easier.  Of course, you don't need to attend college—but going will take what you already know and spin it out in a thousand directions. It will also tell you a million things that you *don't* know. It will introduce you to hundreds of people like you—and hundreds who are different.

The world is a big place, and going to college can be your first step. But to be ready for college you should enjoy learning, discussing ideas and events, taking inquiries one step further, having others listen to you, and sharing with them your additional thoughts.

College will open up possibilities for your future that you may not have otherwise. There are over three thousand institutions of higher learning in the US, ranging in size from a large state university with over forty thousand students to a tiny college that has fewer than thirty.

CHOOSE WELL.

# WHAT MAKES THIS GUIDE DIFFERENT?

I will guide you through a learning process that tells you:

* What to look for in a school.
* What makes a "good" college.
* How to be the best applicant you can be.
* What colleges are looking for.
* How colleges decide who gets admitted.

I intend to cut through the mythology and give you the best information possible. This means no helicopter-parenting and no dive-bomber parenting. I want you, the applicant, to select the colleges to which you will apply and get through the experience of attending college while accruing as little debt as possible.

First, you will need to have a serious talk with your parents or other adults who are in charge of family financial matters. You must know, by at least your sophomore year of high school, about your family's money situation: income, debt, investments, and other financial components.

**Ninth grade is a good time to start thinking about college.** It's the time to start taking education seriously if you haven't before. By "seriously," I mean that you ought to take the information your teachers give you, think about it, look at its perspective, and see how it fits into your overall understanding. Reading books and magazine articles, listening to podcasts, and finding items of interest on the internet can extend your understanding even further. In this way, you will make yourself well informed and college-ready.

# WHY DO YOU WANT TO GO TO COLLEGE?

* To expand your world-view?
* To develop the skills that will help you get a decent job?
* To obtain guidance about which career path to follow?
* To meet others in your peer group who share your ideas?
* To meet others who have opposing ideas?
* To obtain a credential that can help you?
* To get away from home?

All of these reasons are valid. Most people who apply to college are seventeen or eighteen years old. But people mature at different rates. How can you know, for sure, which college to attend or what career you want at that age? You might know your career path now, or you just might enjoy the idea of exploring knowledge for its own sake.

This is all well and good if you don't have to worry about money. If you do, you might need some extra time to decide. A "gap year" of working is a good possibility to consider for anyone who is undecided about a career. You might see that, after all, a college degree is a basic requirement for an entry-level job in the field you want to enter.

There are plenty of good reasons not to go to college, but if you can afford it or can get sufficient financial aid to cover your expenses, college is a wonderful way to spend four years opening your mind to new information and meeting hundreds of additional people who will have an effect on your thinking and experience.

If you are not now prepared for four years of full-time college, there are a number of alternatives:

* You can attend a local community college, saving on living expenses and tuition for two years while taking basic courses that will transfer to a four-year university.

* You can begin working in your chosen field and see what the opportunities are—and whether this field is even right for you.

* You can take a year off to "shadow" a profession-al or have an internship to see what the work-place is like.

But if you want to go right to college after high school, then you have to consider your opportunities.

# THE COLLEGE FRENZY

America seems dominated by a belief that going to a college of a certain caliber is a guarantee of success. Yes, going to a college of a certain caliber can stimulate other factors, such as an appreciation of politics or biology or the importance of learning another language—but these can be accessible at other venues as well.

In the last thirty years or so, going to college has become a mega-major topic affecting millions of people, not only students and professors, but also the countless numbers of people who make money from the college-bound segment of the population: advisors and counselors, administrators, tutors, testing companies, media companies, organizations that offer memberships to those seeking careers, writing centers, summer academies, entrepreneurs, and souvenir manufacturers. (After all, what would visiting a campus mean without swag?)

Other companies, having bought address lists or solicited teachers to nominate "candidates," offer "enrichment programs" to develop "leadership"— for several thousand dollars. Colleges themselves have discovered that offering classes to high school students is big business. These are expensive (especially at private colleges), but students flock to them each summer, hoping that taking a class at **X** will boost their chances of eventually being admitted to **X** (despite messages from **X** that it will not affect applications).

What all the "get into a top-ranked school/major/program" books don't tell you is that there are many things leading to eventual success in life and in your profession. These can depend upon an individual's ability to:

✽ Be sociable.

✽ Make connections with influential people.

✽ Ask the right questions.

✽ Get the attention of important individuals.

✽ Create a record of significant accomplishments.

✽ Be active rather than passive.

These are all positive qualities and can be developed whether or not you are in college.

Many teens spend as much—or more— time preparing or strategizing for college admission than they will actually spend in college. That is so sad and unnecessary. All you need is this book.

If you have chosen to go to college, you must be a curious, diligent student. Your mind must be a sponge, taking in everything that comes your way. There is no substitute for hard work, and real education is work.

If you are a chronic reader, you will do better in preparatory work, for instance, in the verbal sections of standardized exams like the PSAT, SAT, and ACT. And if you do well in advanced math courses, you will do better in the mathematical sections of these same standardized exams.

The better you do in high school courses that seem at first difficult, the better your chances in this process. The better you do in school, the more chances you have of receiving a scholarship or grant.

College can certainly enhance your experiences and appreciation of others, not to mention gaining higher lifetime earnings. The college years typically occur when participants are between the ages of eighteen and twenty-two—a very important period of receptivity to new ideas and experiences. What happens during that time can be life-changing and valuable. However, not going to college as a young adult can certainly be compensated for by professional experiences or military service, for example.

As I said earlier, going to a specific school is no guarantee of happiness or career success. With this in mind, you can address the topic of college holistically. And you need to be aware of:

✱ Things you can't control.
✱ Things you can control.

**You can't control how many others are competing with you in the applicant pool**. The more students competing for a fixed number of admission slots, the harder it is for any individual to be admitted. Look at the acceptance rates for colleges and you will see a reflection of this competitiveness. For instance, although students are aware that a small number of private colleges are the hardest to get into, tens of thousands apply each year, so the number of rejections grows. As a result, these schools have gone from an acceptance rate of 10 or 11 percent—already very competitive—to 5 or 6 percent. For every student admitted, there are probably twenty just as qualified. There is nothing you can do about this.

Likewise, **there is nothing you can do about a school's institutional goals**. Every college and university has a set of goals it would like to reach, and some may change from year to year, but they will not publicize their goals. Some of the goals are in the mission statement on the college website, but others are not mentioned in published sites. For instance, a school may decide to focus on admitting more male students or more females from the Midwest.

Save your efforts for things you <u>can</u> control:

* Your academic record.
* The activities you join and the effort you devote to them.
* Your reading.
* What you write in your essay(s).
* Your relationships with your recommenders.
* Where you choose to apply.

Choosing a college takes a tremendous amount of time and effort. Therefore, **you should start your research in your junior year of high school**.

# YOUR BASIC QUESTIONS

* Where should I apply?
* When should I apply?
* What are my chances of being admitted?
* How am I going to pay for four or five years of college?

# AND ASK YOURSELF:

* Why has tuition risen at twice the rate of inflation?
* Why is student debt the greatest it has ever been?
* Why are there so many well-paid administrators?
* What is the effect on students of the overuse of contingent faculty?

These are questions you may not have considered before, but they are important ones. Talk them over with your parents and guidance counselors.

**And a warning:** Do not apply for Early Decision, Early Decision I, or Early Decision II, unless you are very, very sure. If the school accepts you, this decision is <u>binding</u>.

You may wish to consider applying before the Early Action deadline though. This is <u>not binding</u>.

# HOW TO CHOOSE WHERE TO APPLY

There are many factors influencing your decision:

* Where you live.
* Where you go to school.
* Your family history.
* Your family obligations.
* How much money your family has.

Over the years, I have heard parents and students say these unrealistic things:

* "I want my son to go to the most prestigious school he can get into."
* "I am expected to go to engineering school because my father is an engineer, and so was *his* father."
* "You need to get into an Ivy. Any Ivy. These are the most prestigious schools!"
* "Our daughter is our family's last hope. She has to get into _____."
* "Either you get into a top-ranked school, or you're going to community college."
* "You were admitted to *where*? Our dog could get in there!"

These demands and opinions are incredibly unfair to applicants. They minimize the applicant's dreams, they overemphasize a narrow band of schools, and they equate "success" with certain fields of study or certain schools. The information provided in this guide can save you from these mistakes.

# CRAFTiNG A PRELiMiNARY CoLLEGE LiST

✱ What is most important to you—prestige or practicality? Are you looking for a "name" college or one that will give you a solid preparation in, say, the basics of finance? The "name" college may provide both—but it will come at a higher financial cost and increased pressure.

✱ Do you want a school that is near your home? In the same state? As far away as possible?

✱ Would you like to go to school in a large city? Near a large city? In a small town?

✱ Do you want to be surrounded by people who are like you? Or do you prefer a mix of people, cultures, religions, beliefs?

✱ Do you want there to be a sports program? Do you wish to participate, or watch?

✱ Do you want to live at school in a dorm or in an off-campus apartment with roommates?

✱ How much is this going to cost?

# THESE THINGS ARE <u>TRUE</u> ABOUT COLLEGE ADMISSION:

* They accept students who are most likely to <u>enroll</u>.
* You don't necessarily have to be #1 at your high school to get accepted.
* There isn't a magic GPA that anyone has to have.
* Likewise, there isn't any specific score on the SAT or ACT that you must have.
* You will need <u>an ally on your high school faculty</u>—a counselor, teacher, or someone else who wants to see you succeed.
* You will need <u>an ally in the admissions office</u>—a rep with whom you clicked, someone you met when you visited, someone who remembers you and with whom you have established a rapport. There will be one or two of these people in your search as you narrow down your choices. You can write to these people, but not often. You cannot be a pest. Choose carefully.
* College decisions may appear illogical.
* A college admits those they want to admit.

And in the world of college admissions, remember this:

# "IT ALL DEPENDS."

This is often cited by admissions readers and college advisors. Admissions is not a scientific procedure, with right or wrong answers.

# HOW TO ASSESS A COLLEGE

Teachers worry about their students' futures: Have they been prepared for college? Will they be able to afford their education? Will they be forced to take on years of crushing debt? These fears are based in reality. The COVID pandemic of 2020-2022 has brought long-standing inequities in the educational system to the forefront. College administrators remain devoted to the popularity contest of ranking, to see if they are among the "Top 10" or "Top 100."

**Forget the rankings.** Years ago, I met someone on the staff of a certain news magazine that had the first college "rankings." When I accused his publication of starting a national frenzy about college, he responded, "It put bread on the table." It was a marketing plan that worked—for a while.

But it started hysterics about "how is my school ranked?" This led to colleges fudging or creating statistics that would raise their profiles. Rankings are just popularity contests based on all kinds of factors. You may see that one school says "ranked #1 nationally," only to find out that this ranking refers to something (for example, the length of its pool) that does not impact you, as a prospective student, at all.

You need to do thorough research, which includes going to college fairs sponsored by your school, nearby college fairs, and campus tours (if you can afford to travel to those schools). Talk with trusted friends and teachers. Spend your junior year of high school thinking in general about college and gathering information. Get specific as you enter your senior year.

# THE ALTERNATIVE TOUR

Take the official tour at a nearby college, even if you don't want to attend. See how things are done. What questions occur to you? Do admissions staff give you thoughtful answers or do they seem more interested in gathering applications? If you are interested in a school, you will want to go on an official tour. Go, and listen well. But please remember that the goal of a good tour is to make students want to apply.

After you have taken the official tour sponsored by the college, go back for another visit and see things in more depth and at your own pace. Here are some suggestions:

* If possible, go into a classroom building you didn't see on the official tour; check the rooms' condition.

* Go into the student union and look at the notice boards. Are they recent? Any things coming up? Concerts, films, discussions? Will they take place on campus, or off?

* Have a meal or snack in the dining hall. Does the display appeal to you? Is there a healthy buzz (people talking to one another), chaotic noise, or

near-silence? What about the quality of the food, and what choices were you offered?

* Talk to some <u>current students</u>. Are they happy they came here? What was the deciding factor in their choice?

* *Note: only try this on a non-rainy day.* Sit in a <u>high-traffic area on the campus</u>, such as in front of the library, student union, or dining hall. Stay at least half an hour. Do most students look happy? Is there interaction between them? Do teachers seem to be conversing with students? Are students in groups or by themselves? You can learn a lot about the "campus climate" just by watching.

* Look at the <u>bumper stickers and decals</u> on student cars. What causes do they support? Do they say anything negative? Do they seem to suggest any sort of political or cultural stance? *To ensure your safety, do this with a parent or another adult, as it involves being in parking lots, which are often active with traffic.*

* Is this <u>a safe campus</u>? Again, *do this with a parent or other adult.* Go back at dusk and walk around until it's dark. Do you feel safe? Are there other students out and about, or is the campus deserted? Is the campus well lit, and do you see evidence of a safety system?

* Pick up a copy of the <u>campus newspaper</u> or read it online, and see what the main articles are about. What seem to be the major issues at this school?

* Go to the <u>career center</u> and ask a counselor there about what jobs are offered to students. Which employers are coming to the school to interview students? Are the displays current? What is the physical condition and staff size of the career center? It is likely that this office will be very important to you as an enrolled student as you seek career advice, internships, part-time jobs, and employment after graduation.

* Check the <u>campus website</u> frequently. What's going on at the school? Read the school's own social media. Again, you will be able to get a feeling of the "vibe" of the school.

* What seems to be the <u>stress level</u> of the college? Are de-stressing activities held?

* Does the school have <u>first-rate medical care</u> for students? How about <u>mental health care</u>?

You can repeat these experiences later at schools where you are a serious applicant.

# ABOUT THOSE TEST SCORES

*The Big Test: The Secret History of the American Meritocracy* was published by Nicholas Lemann in 1999, examining the origins of the Educational Testing Service and the SAT. ETS was founded in 1948 and for decades followed the opinions of James Bryant Conant and Henry Chauncey in crafting the SAT. Lemann's book gained major attention because it showed ETS's purpose was to "test more rather than to ponder the merits of testing." There are all kinds of accusations against the SAT. First of all, success on the test has been linked to those with financial and other advantages. Applicants who grow up familiar with books and music, with art and science; who have had their reasoning processes challenged; and who constantly challenge themselves tend to do better on these exams than others. **High test scores are often—<u>but not always</u>—linked with financial advantage.** Add to this the proliferation of test prep books, test prep services, and private college consultants, and success on the tests seems definitely linked to money.

And the university "enrichment" programs, designed to give students exposure to science, medicine, the arts, history, and a chance to experience life on a campus, all cost a lot of money. Some programs include test preparation. These programs may or may not give students an advantage when it comes to college applications or test results.

It is possible, though, to beat the stress and pressure that goes along with the tests.

✴ You can choose the ACT instead. More people know about the SAT than the ACT, but they are similar. One type of test does not "look better" than the other.

✴ You can apply to "test optional" schools. Naturally, without test scores, something else will be stressed more. It might be the essay. It might be recommendations. It will depend on the school. If the college policy says "test optional," it is truly test optional. If application instructions give you a choice to send your scores, only send them if they are high. That means for the SAT a combined score of 1450 and up and for the ACT a score of 34 or higher.

✴ Test prep companies will promise to raise your score by 100 points on the SAT. But most students who take the tests for their second time as seniors have higher scores anyway. They are older, they have learned more, and they have absorbed more knowledge. A test prep course will give you some familiarity with the format of the test and some test-taking tips. But your overall score may or may not change.

✳ You can start your education at a two-year institution, which typically does not ask for either the SAT or ACT. You can then apply to transfer to a four-year institution in your second year without having to submit test scores.

✳ If you have taken AP courses in high school, you should send any score of 3 or higher. If you don't send them, colleges will assume that you took the courses but opted out of the tests, or you did take them and scored poorly on all of them.

✳ Please do not think of any test score as defining you. Ask your teachers or other adults what their scores were. Bet no one even remembers.

# WHAT CHARACTERIZES A "GOOD" COLLEGE?

When students ask counselors to compile a list of recommended colleges, they are often thinking of rank and reputation. But, as stated previously, magazine rankings are usually just a popularity contest and sometimes are not always even true. Ranking can also make admission rates vary; colleges have learned to manipulate rankings without fundamentally changing anything about their schools. Some counselors, overburdened with having to provide lists for several hundred students, simply recommend colleges they have relied on in the past: their own schools, local favorites, colleges that come to visit their high schools.

**Don't limit yourself.** Looking at these institutions is beneficial, but many truly good colleges are overlooked. Therefore, utilizing additional measures can provide real, significant information about an institution's quality.

* What is its retention rate? What percentage of first-year students return to this campus for their second year?
* What is its acceptance rate? You might not want to apply to a school that accepts only 5 percent

of its applicants, but a school that accepts 95 percent is not very selective.

✱ What is its four-year <u>graduation</u> rate? Six-year graduation rate?

✱ The school may offer the major a student wants, but <u>how many courses</u> are offered? Are there research opportunities or summer internships for undergraduates?

✱ What is the average <u>class size</u>? What is the overall student-faculty ratio? And exactly who—full-time faculty, graduate students, adjuncts—is doing the teaching?

All of the answers may be found in the statistics for each school, which are published in the **Common Data Set**.

# WHAT IS THE COMMON DATA SET?

The Common Data Set, or CDS, allows comparisons among colleges and universities. It is a document of about thirty-three pages compiled annually by each school's office of institutional research. It is uniform, meaning that the same information is asked of each school in the same order. Colleges and universities, however, are not required to enter their data.

**The CDS offers a wealth of statistics.** Who is reporting the information? Does the school offers undergraduate degrees only or both undergraduate and graduate degrees? How many applications are filed each year? How many are chosen? And how many have enrolled? Does the school offer a waiting list? The total number of enrolled students is given: how many men, how many women. It tells how many teachers there are and what their highest degree is. You can see the sticker price (that is, tuition charged before scholarships and financial aid are taken into consideration), the cost of housing and dining, and additional fees charged.

Colleges know that not every person is looking for every fact, so their websites often give a page of "fast facts" about themselves. There should also be a link to the current Common Data Set; most schools give the last few years' results. This way, you can see in what ways the school has expanded or not. But the first thing to look for is whether the school's website even offers a link to the Common Data Set.

You may need to go to the school's "search" function and simply ask for the CDS. The key is to locate it. Not every school makes the CDS visible. If there are just "Fast Facts," use a search engine, entering the name of the school AND the phrase "Common Data Set." Either it will or won't come up. You may be led to a "CDS" produced by another source, with some of the data available. Or you may be asked to fill out a data request form. Or you may be told to request information from a certain person on campus. This requires a time investment and may not provide the information you seek.

To find the most valuable information the CDS has to offer, you need to look for the college's selectivity (that is, the percent of applicants that are accepted), retention rate, graduation rate, and the number of faculty teaching.

# YOUR RESEARCH

For every school you are considering, note its selectivity, retention, graduation rate, supportiveness, and faculty working conditions.

**✷ How selective are the schools you are looking at?**

| | Acceptance Rate |
|---|---|
| Most Selective | 3%–4% |
| Highly selective | 5%–10% |
| Selective | 11%–19% |
| Fairly selective | 20%–29% |
| Moderately selective | 30%–49% |
| Somewhat selective | 50%–59% |
| Less selective | 60%–79% |
| Non-selective | 80% or more |

*Note: State universities have a preference for in-state residents and will usually have two different acceptance rates, one for in-state applicants and one for out-of-state.*

✱ **Take a look at retention.** What percentage of first-year students return to this school for a second year? A rate of 97 percent is excellent. But 65 percent says something else. A quite popular school has a figure of 85 percent. (I located this information after a bit of digging.) There can be many reasons for students not returning, including health and finances. You need to ask the admissions office for an explanation.

✱ **Next, look at the school's six-year graduation rate**. The CDS gives this as an indication of student success. A six-year rate is often given, rather than four, as many factors can interfere with student progress: internships, illness, family reasons, switching majors, or holding down a job while balancing school responsibilities. If, for example, *every* member of a cohort that began college in the fall of 2020 graduated by the spring of 2024, that would be a rate of 100 percent. No college has that. But 91 percent is pretty good. 42 percent is not. What if you can't find the graduation rate? It's there: colleges know this information. You will need to ask.

* **Is there sufficient support for a course of study?** If you want a certain major, it's easy to find out which schools have them. But how many courses does the school offer? What is their size? Does the department help students get internships? Is there a space for students to gather? How many majors graduate each year? What are last year's graduates doing?  Schools will be eager to provide data about successful graduates. You will need to ask, especially at the office of career services.

* **Significantly, who teaches the courses?** Who teaches the introductory courses and who teaches more advanced classes? This is the final, and possibly the most significant, question you can ask about each college or university. The next section explains why this is so.

# WHO IS DOING THE TEACHING?

This question is critically important. The answer will be different for colleges and universities. A university has a graduate program, and these usually assign advanced students to teach introductory courses and some electives. All of us who have been graduate students have had this experience. But more and more, colleges are trying to save money, and that means cutting expenses, such as paying teachers and updating equipment.

You may read in a college's or university's promotional materials about a famous professor who is there. But what are your chances of having this professor for a class? It depends upon the school. Some will have their undergraduates taught by graduate students only. Some may have full professors teaching first-year students. You will need to inquire.

It is normal for universities to have about 20 to 30 percent of its teaching staff be part-time employees, reflecting the use of graduate students as teachers. Students who choose to attend a university should expect this situation. But it is not normal to have all the undergraduate classes taught by graduate students, leaving graduate courses for the professors. It is <u>not normal</u> for a college, which has no graduate school, to have a huge percentage of its courses taught by part-time instructors.

It is <u>not normal</u> to have 40 percent, 50 percent, 60 percent or more of the teaching staff working as part-time or contingent faculty. "Contingent" means that these teachers' work is contingent upon the need of the school. Part-time teachers are called many things: adjuncts, part-time teachers, part-time professors, and contingent labor. They can comprise anywhere between 4 percent and 72 percent of an institution's faculty. At some schools, contingent labor accounts for as many as 40 to 50 percent of the teaching staff.

While some schools may have low overall percentages of part-time faculty, some of their departments offer undergraduate courses taught primarily by contingent labor. These teachers are generally paid much less than regular faculty, often work without contracts or benefits, and do not know their teaching assignments until the last minute. But because they are cheaper to hire, many schools use them extensively.  Or a college or university may hire a teacher full-time—but only for one year. You will need to look at the school's teaching assignments very carefully.

It is definitely <u>not normal</u> for a school to have more part-time teachers than full-time teachers—and yet this condition often exists. The result is a huge labor issue that definitely affects students' learning. A dissatisfied faculty or graduate-student labor force can reflect working conditions that affect students' learning conditions. And a constantly changing faculty denies students an atmosphere of reliability. Part-time teachers are not necessarily bad, just as full-time, tenured teachers are not necessarily good. But having a large number of contingent faculty also means less contact time per student.

Which campuses have seen repeated, chronic labor issues? Look up labor actions on campus. Ask current students at the schools you are considering if they are satisfied with the teaching there, as well as access to their instructors. The constant search for work by these instructors and the resultant revolving door is harmful to the student experience.

The Common Data Set can provide you with this information, for it lists how many full-time teachers a school has and how many part-time. The answer is always in part I (as in I, J, K). The CDS is not flaw-less, however. It does not distinguish between the types of part-time teachers. (An instructor may work full-time elsewhere and also teach one college class; or the instructor may teach one class and work part-time at two more schools.) To learn the truth, your counselors and you must ask, "What is the percentage of undergraduate courses taught by part-time faculty?"

Prospective students must ask very pointed questions. When colleges send admissions reps to high schools to recruit applicants, they answer most questions. But they don't address the working conditions of faculty; in fact, they are usually unaware of them. Those who admit students and those who hire those students' teachers usually have nothing to do with one another. Sometimes, often at smaller schools, faculty and administration do work together for the benefit of the students, but those are the exceptions.

Still, any school (except those with special circumstances) hiring more than half its faculty on a contingent basis is either in financial trouble or is a questionable employer. This can be a huge factor in choosing a college. The growing reliance on contingent college faculty is a significant issue in higher education and is a pervasive problem nationally. If a school doesn't care about its teachers, how can it care about its students? Some colleges may charge high tuition yet shortchange their students. Students may obtain a degree but not necessarily gain a real education.

Students today must be very thoughtful and ask many questions—some of which may make you and others feel uncomfortable. But they are necessary—your education and career may depend on these answers.

# MAKE SURE YOUR LIST IS VARIED

Once you have built your preliminary college list, you still have a lot of work ahead of you. You know which colleges are promoted by your high school. You know which are the most-applied-to schools. And you know from promotional materials and the college's website what it says about itself. Now you need to get the facts, and that means hours of research. If you plan to visit, do your research before you go. You will get more out of time on campus.

**You should apply to about eight to ten schools**, of different sizes and rigor, with different acceptance rates, but you should be excited about the prospect of attending each of them. You don't know where you may be admitted, so to offset disappointment, you should be willing to enroll at and feel good about attending any of the schools on your list.

People think that if they apply to twenty schools they will improve their odds of admission. But if you choose the schools carefully, you will need to apply to only eight to ten. Don't dismiss local colleges, but expand your search. Do keep in mind the cost of each application. You may want to apply to even fewer.

Now make a list reflecting the schools where you think you want to apply.
* How many schools are there?
* How do they differ?
* What is the graduation rate?
* What is the cost? (Remember to include transportation to and from distant schools.)

These are the main types of schools:
* State (public) universities and colleges.
* Private universities and colleges.
* Religiously affiliated universities and colleges.
* Community colleges or two-year schools.
* Online universities and for-profit schools (the ones with TV and internet ads). *Avoid these!*

Most schools are "not for profit"—but that has nothing to do with how much you will pay for a degree. <u>Avoid any schools that are for profit.</u> Profit status is generally stated on school websites; you can investigate the problems with for-profit schools on the internet.

# IMPORTANT THINGS TO CONSIDER ABOUT THE SCHOOLS TO WHICH YOU APPLY

This is what is meant by a "diverse" list of colleges. You should have one or two schools of each kind.

* **A "reach" school.** This is a college or university that has an extremely rigorous reputation and to which entry is very, very limited. An experienced counselor will have a good idea of which schools will be a challenge. All schools can surprise with their decision-making. But unless applicants want to collect rejection letters, they should limit this type of application to one or two.

* **A "hidden gem" school.** These are likely to be in less-populated areas and small in size. They may be public or private. If they are in less populated areas, life will center around the school and the teachers will be more likely to devote themselves to the students. At smaller schools, classes should be smaller. Look at schools with total enrollments of under 2,000. But apply all the criteria you would to larger institutions.

* **A larger state university or one of its branches.** Every state has a university system that it supports. These range from affordable to very

expensive and may have a different acceptance and tuition rate for in-state and out-of-state applicants. Programs are generally good, and the best students continue to graduate school, medical or law school, or MBA programs.

* **A less-demanding school but one which has a solid academic reputation.** This is a school where you are likely to be accepted. Avoid thinking of it as a "safety school." This term has often been used to imply that an applicant is certain to be accepted. Remember that what is a "safety" for one applicant may be a "reach" for another. Students should think that they want to attend all the schools on their list. Some students tend to have little respect for schools thought of as "safeties" and somehow that is conveyed in their applications. If colleges that feel they are relied upon as "safeties"—if an applicant's profile is way above the average for the school—then they may not consider this applicant a serious candidate. But they won't deny non-serious candidates straightaway; more likely, they will banish them to a waitlist which will never move.

Be aware that some schools try to get by on past reputations. Their publicity often cites past glories and ignores current data. Look closely at the number of full-time faculty it presently has as opposed to what it used to have. Is it trying to save money while skimping on attention to students? Look for the prominence of recent graduates, as opposed to the fame of alumni from thirty or forty years ago. Have they kept up with infrastructure? Are classrooms up-to-date?

And what is an indication that the school is to be avoided? Look closely at the faculty and graduates. Is the school's career center open and honest about the success of its graduates?

# CHECKLIST FOR YOUR COLLEGES

Now that you have created your list of appropriate colleges, how many of these can you answer in the affirmative?

* Does this school have <u>a good academic reputation</u>? What is your source of information?

* Is this <u>primarily an undergraduate school</u>, or is it <u>known for its graduate programs</u>?

* Are there <u>courses</u> in the catalog that excite you? Are they on a regular schedule (some classes are offered, for example, every other year)? Who is teaching them?

* What is the <u>political atmosphere</u>? Does it make you feel comfortable, uncomfortable, challenged, content?

* Do the <u>graduates have a successful record of decent employment</u>? What is the level of job satisfaction of these graduates?

* Does it have <u>an active career center</u> and does it bring employers to campus? How many students find employment through the career center?

* What about <u>the advisory system</u>? How many times a year can a student go to see their advisor? What is the average length of employment of the advisors?

* How easy is it to get into the <u>courses you will need</u> for transfers or graduation?

* What is the <u>average class size</u>?

* Are the teachers <u>full-time faculty</u>? If there is part-time faculty, what percentage of undergraduate classes does it teach?

* Is there enough <u>housing on campus</u>? Is campus housing in good condition? Did you see a sample dorm room on your tour?

* Is there a <u>good way to get around campus</u>? Is there reliable transportation to the nearest city? The airport?

* Are there <u>extracurricular activities</u> you would enjoy?

* Will you feel <u>comfortable</u> on this campus?

* Will you feel <u>safe</u>—physically and emotionally? What security measures are in place?

* Is there a certain population with whom you identify? Are there groups of <u>people like you</u>? Are you satisfied about how well you are represented on this campus?

* Is the <u>campus food</u> appealing? Is there care shown for those with special dietary needs (e.g., allergic sensitivities, kosher or halal meals, vegetarian or vegan options)?

* Is this school <u>affordable</u>? Check your FAFSA

profile. Have you been offered a scholarship, or will you be expected to pay an exorbitant amount on a school loan for a very long time?

# NOW you ARE READY To CREATE your FiNAL LiST

When you have narrowed your choices and completed your final list, you are ready to apply.

**Your high school transcript.** This will be asked for by any college to which you apply. They may at first ask you to self-report your grades. Later they will ask for an official transcript. What you report should be the same as what your official transcript says you earned. You will be judged against other students in your school. When I say that actual GPA doesn't matter, I mean that the courses you take count more. What if a high school offers AP classes, but a student who has avoided these gets a higher GPA? What matters is the curriculum you select. If your high school does not offer AP or honors classes, which are often more difficult, you will not be penalized. But every high school has challenging courses. And colleges like to see that you have agreed to take on academic rigor and are prepared to do work on a university level.

**Parts of the application.** Each of these will be explained in more detail.

* The application form itself (including extracurriculars, activities, teams, clubs).
* Standardized test scores (SAT, ACT, AP results), if required.
* The essay or essays.
* The interview, if one is given.
* Your counselor's recommendation.
* Other recommendations.

# THE APPLICATION FORM

The **Common Application** requires the same standard information from every applicant. It is used by over a thousand colleges and universities; other colleges will use their own forms. The good thing is that it allows you to apply to many schools simultaneously, so you don't have to give the same information over and over. The negative is that it allows you to apply to too many colleges and doesn't make you narrow your choices.

The Common Application explains everything in great detail. It will also let you set up a practice account so you can gain familiarity with the forms.

There will be a section about your in-school and out-of-class activities. Everyone's list is different. There are no "prestige" activities, as one parent demanded to know when I was working in university admissions. Do what you love. Avoid "pay to play" activities, where students are offered access and opportunity for a price. Better to devise activities (such as tutoring neighborhood kids or running a program to visit shut-ins) on your own. Expect many questions about your family background. You do not have to reveal everything. You can leave out race and ethnic background if this makes you uncomfortable.

If you are comfortable revealing challenges, impediments to learning, or other factors that have been in your way as you have gone through school and life, the essay is your chance to tell about them.

# TEST SCORES

Read the testing section of the Common App very carefully. You will be asked to self-report your scores if you want them counted. *(See the section of this guide about standardized tests.)*

# THE PERSONAL STATEMENT OR ESSAY

As the only part of the entire application where you get to speak for yourself, the "personal statement" or essay is <u>absolutely crucial</u>. There is a 650-word limit (with a 250-word minimum). Do not aim for the minimum. This doesn't mean you have to go into panic mode or consult writing experts or attend essay workshops.

What it does mean is that this is an opportunity you ought to use well. No matter which prompt you answer, they really are all the same: <u>tell us about yourself</u>.

The best essays give a glimpse into the life of an applicant. It does not have to make a reader weep or laugh, but it does need to be <u>real</u>, <u>correctly written</u>, and <u>make a clear point</u>.

**Do:**
* Tell a story in which you are an important character.
* Vary the openings of each paragraph.
* Write correctly, without abbreviations or slang.

* Refer to a specific incident or incidents (without giving names, of course).

**Don't:**
* Begin with a quotation. (This is such a cliché.)
* Use abbreviations unless they stand for something well understood (Dr., etc., Mr.).
* Say how much you want to go to _____ College. They don't care. Instead, give them a reason to want you in their student body.
* Write so much about another person or people that you neglect to tell about yourself.
* Say how great you are—they should figure that out from what you write!
* Plagiarize—presenting someone else's words as your own. This can lead to an automatic denial.
* Use AI-generated essays—there are ways colleges can tell.

It's fine to start your first draft wherever you are. It can be the middle of a story. But you have to think of something from your life that actually occurred (and ought to be fairly recent). Choose an event or encounter that affected you deeply, that helped to create the person you are today (who will not be the same person in 20 years). What happened? In what ways has its impact lasted?

**Topics to avoid:**

✱ How stressed out you are.

✱ How privileged you are.

✱ Complaints about your parents, your school, your teachers. You will come across as disgruntled, whiny, and unappealing.

✱ What you were great at before you attended high school.

✱ The essay itself and how it just adds to the pressure you are under. ("Here I am, sitting at my desk an hour before the application is due, trying to decide what to tell you...")

Writing about COVID will get old, but not in every case. A special opportunity is available if you speak about how it affected you, and how you coped with it.

**Use your natural voice.** Do not sound like a walking dictionary or thesaurus. The saying in the admissions world is "if it sounds like it was written by a forty-five-year-old lawyer, it was probably written by a forty-five-year-old lawyer." Going to an outside writing coach or tutor—who may or may not even write a good part of the essay—is often unhelpful "help." You think admissions personnel can't tell when an essay is just too polished? They are very experienced, and usually can tell when something does not add up. It is often obvious when an application seems "packaged."

The very best essays sound like they were composed by teens. In fact, the most successful essays are written by teenagers. Yes, there are AI chatbots that can write essays. Colleges have figured out how to deal with this. Adults wishing to offer genuine help can do so by reading the essay but should refrain from anything other than pointing out severe writing errors or unclear ideas. All those "winning essay" books are not that important—they are about others' experiences, not yours. Write sincerely about yourself, with details and examples to add color and clarity. <u>Remember, the whole purpose is to make the reader get to know you personally.</u>

**Some ideas:**
* Are there family stories, grandparents' adventures, tales about your family's home country, etc., that you have grown up hearing? How has learning about these stories affected you and the way you have developed?
* Have you ever been pushed to conform to something you did not like? Have you ever behaved a certain way or done a certain thing to impress someone else? Describe what you did and your

feelings about it. How did things work out? What did you learn from the experience?

✱ Some people want to win—an argument, a game, a contest, a leadership position—at any cost. Write about a time when you were in, or observed, such a situation. How did it turn out? What did you learn from this?

✱ Write about a family you have observed, whether yours or a friend's. What seems to bind a family together—or push them apart? Are their clear gender roles in the family? What have they modeled for you in terms of relationship dynamics? Is there anyone you admire more than others, and why?

# OTHER ESSAYS

You may or may not be asked to write additional essays by the schools to which you are applying. In all cases, write genuinely, tell the truth, and explain yourself clearly. It is perfectly permissible to have someone check your writing to make sure it is error-free—but it is not okay for them to write or rewrite your essay.

# THE INTERVIEW

Comparatively few colleges or universities ask for interviews. With thousands of applicants, they simply do not have time. But some require them, while others recommend an interview. If you apply to a school that offers one, just answer truthfully. Admissions decisions are made on the basis of other criteria, not on an interview alone.

# OTHER MYTHS ABOUT COLLEGE ADMISSION

✱ <u>You do not have to have an internship.</u> But you should have a record of activities, and you should show that you have devoted serious time to one or more things. As mentioned earlier, "pay to play" activities (where you pay a fee) should be avoided.

✱ <u>You do not have to have community service.</u> You just need to show an interest in others. You do not need to go anywhere exotic (at your own expense). Doing something for others right in your neighborhood is fine.

✱ <u>You do not have to be a member of a "national" honor group.</u> A group that charges for membership is not an honor. Honors are given, not paid for.

✱ <u>You do not have to have a resume.</u> But you might want a record of your accomplishments and activities for yourself.

# RECOMMENDATIONS

**Colleges will want to know what to expect from you.** Your school counselor will probably write a letter about you gleaned either from what you tell them or from your teachers. If you attend a small private school, this letter will be individualized. If you go to a large urban school, **it is your responsibility to make your counselor aware of your dreams, abilities, and accomplishments**. You should make an appointment with your high school counselor during your junior year, and again near the beginning of your senior year.

You will probably be required to include two teacher recommendations to indicate how well you may do in academic subjects. These will include your English, math, foreign language, history, and science teachers. Do not use coaches or advisors; they may serve as supplemental recommenders. And do not ask any recommenders at the last minute! Give them time to write thoughtful letters.

**Pick teachers who know you well.** They might not teach a class in which you are getting the best grades, but they should know you. The most effective recommendations will give admissions readers a glimpse of what they can expect from you in the classroom. A brief recommendation that states you are an excellent student who maintains a B+ average in a course is useless because it is not specific enough and does not go into any depth about who you are as a student.

A strong and useful recommendation is one that mentions that you:

✳ Ask good questions that initiate class discussion.

✳ Are most interested in the "why?" of an issue.

✳ May not always have the top grade in the course but maintain constantly improving grades and make the writer glad to have become a teacher—this is significant.

If a teacher asks for your resume, politely ask what's the use of this teacher's mentioning your other activities. A history or science teacher who sees you five times a week in class should be able to write a detailed letter. The college just needs to get an idea of what type of student you will be.

Some colleges ask for supplemental recommendations. In that case, a letter from a coach, advisor, youth leader, teacher of a class you are taking outside of high school, or employer will serve just fine. Are there more prestigious letters? Does a letter from your local senator carry more weight than an employer who can attest to your honesty and work ethic? No. Likewise, will a letter from an alumnus or alumna help? Only if this person knows you very well and can honestly address all the issues that a strong teacher recommendation does.

# WILL I BE ADMITTED?

No ethical college counselor or advisor can state with any certainty that you will be admitted to any specific program at any undergraduate school. You may have to deal with counselors who say "you will likely be accepted" but this is not a guarantee. Sometimes a school that has admitted students in the past—even as recently as last year—with a profile closely resembling yours may change its standards this year.

All counselors—whether you go to a public school, a private school, or have an independent counselor—will give you sincere, solid suggestions. They do not want to see you disappointed.

This book is intended to supplement their knowledge with yours and to give you the added advantage of extra information.

# WHAT DO COLLEGES REALLY WANT?

In general, all colleges want applicants who:
· Have a strong record of academic achievement.
· Show evidence that they have challenged themselves.
· Show genuine interest in learning.
· Show an interest in looking beyond themselves.
· Show that they will add to the life of the college.
· Show "demonstrated interest" in going to a particular college/university. (This may or may not matter.)

**They want well-rounded students who will attend <u>their</u> school.** They want students who are academically qualified, who can do this college's work without much difficulty. No school wants a student to fail. If the school worries that an applicant is not academically qualified, it will reject that student. Enrollment management is of great importance to colleges and universities. They don't want to "waste" an acceptance on a student they are pretty sure will not end up registering. So if you apply to a college where your qualifications greatly exceed those of the usual admitted student, you might find yourself denied or waitlisted.

They want a student body that is diverse. Diverse racially, regionally, by gender, and by interest. If a school admits everyone who is white, whose parents are college-educated, is from Pennsylvania, and plays soccer, that would be pretty boring.

**They want students who will add something to their profile.** This is harder to define. And decisions may seem random or illogical to you. But these students have been accepted for a reason. A student with a lower GPA but who plays the trumpet brilliantly will be a stellar addition to the school band. Likewise the basketball player who never misses a shot. Or a big donor's son being admitted may make it possible for the library to have a new wing.

**Sometimes decisions will seem random and arbitrary. And in some cases they are.** This is especially true of those schools that are competitive. When the admissions office, after getting to the third round of reading applications, still has a thousand from which they can accept only twenty, what do they do? Sometimes there is a human factor: if an application just appeals to one admissions reader, that reader may cast a deciding vote. On the other hand, if something turns off an admissions reader, the decision may turn into a rejection. Colleges will never, ever explain what they do.

I remember one year when I attended a regional post-admissions workshop. "Was it just me," asked one counselor, "or was there a pattern of decisions that seemed unexplainable?" He had a student who was rejected by a large state university, waitlisted by a large private university, and accepted by an Ivy. As it is said about college admissions, "it all depends." But depends upon what? That remains a mystery.

However, in general, the more selective a college or university, the more random the decision may seem to be. It bears repeating: *the more selective the school, the more random the decision will seem.*

# PAYING FOR COLLEGE

College is expensive in this country, but there is a lot of financial aid. So the better a high school student you are, the more colleges and other organizations will be willing to invest in you.

Don't decide where to apply on the basis of cost alone. You will have to wait until you see what financial aid you may receive before making a final decision. <u>If you see that cost is a concern, then go to the best state school you can get into in your home state.</u>

Save additional schooling—a master's or PhD, law school, nursing school, medical or dental school for later. You *can* economize on your undergraduate degree. No one asks where their dentist went for undergraduate studies. They only want to know where their dentist went to dental school.

On the other hand, where you get your undergraduate degree can impact your admission to graduate or professional schools like law or medical schools. You can look ahead to your professional school ambitions as you apply to college, but they should not be the most important factors in your decision.

Unless you come from a family that can pay for all tuition and expenses without any help from scholarships, grants, or loans, you (and those paying for your education) will need to complete the FAFSA form. There is a recently changed edition. Read it thoroughly!

The best outcome, if you can do it, is to be awarded a scholarship. There may be merit scholarships provided by the college. Start investigating early! Next best is a grant. See what awards will come directly from the school. And don't forget private grants, which will come from organizations outside the college, such as the Rotary Club or the Coca-Cola Company. Scholarships and grants are best because they are gifts to you, and they do not have to be repaid. You may have to put in a lot of effort, because $500 will not go far offsetting a $50,000 bill.

If you need a loan, a good source may be the Federal Family Education Loan Program. It is sponsored by the US Department of Education, and you *do* need to repay it. In fact, you will have to start paying interest on it sixty days after completing your degree with at least half-time study. Loans are not scholarships; they do need to be repaid.

Read offers of loans very carefully! Take them to someone experienced with the interpretation of loans. This person may be a lawyer, accountant, or guidance counselor. In many cases, colleges will offer loans that could turn out to be very expensive. First-generation students and students of color are most likely to receive these offers. You may find yourself in debt for many years. Be very careful with anything you sign. Take all forms you receive to someone experienced with these forms!

Before accepting any loan offer, go to the website **understandingfafsa.org**, which will explain how to decipher acceptance and award letters. Make sure to confer with someone who can explain how big your financial burden will be.

# HOW TO RESPOND TO DISAPPOINTING LETTERS

Everyone wants an acceptance letter, and no one wants to receive a "waitlist" letter, which sends a student to a waiting list in the event that a spot becomes available—generally when someone who has been accepted decides not to enroll. It's a very uncomfortable situation to find yourself in, especially because you have a deadline looming for enrollment elsewhere.

Here is where your demonstrated interest (which you have indicated to the person you feel is an "ally" in the admissions office) can come in. You *really* want to go to this school, and you have made this clear in your application. Upon receiving a waitlist letter, write back immediately and remind them of this. This may turn your waitlist status to acceptance. But it may be too late in the process to be considered for any financial aid.

# CONCLUSION

<u>College is a multimillion-dollar business.</u> It is a huge choice that can determine many things about your future: your first job, what part of the country you will live in, who your friends will be. But it is also a vast financial swamp filled with many costs that you don't even know about yet. Fifty years ago, when many of your teachers went to college, the average yearly tuition was $395 at a public college and $1,700 at a private college. Today the average tuition is $25,000—and that is average. Now add room, board, and fees.

<u>The total cost far, far outstrips the rise in the cost of living.</u> And the pursuit of college education generates a lot of money.  Many people make sizable incomes in college-related industries (textbook publishing, food services, think tanks, souvenir marketing, to name a few).

<u>Tread carefully.</u> Know ahead of time approximately what your degree will cost. Be prepared as best you can to apply. Be proactive. Ask questions appropriately. If you follow my suggestions, there should be few surprises. I cannot, of course, guarantee that you will be admitted to any specific college, but you

will be admitted. It just might not be the college where you originally hoped to go! And then you can start living your own dream.

## GOOD LUCK TO YOU!

# HEARTFELT THANKS
## FOR THEIR GUIDANCE TO...

**Marcia Brown Harris**, former director of The Career Center at the University of North Carolina at Chapel Hill, and

**Marjorie Nieuwenhuis**, former director of college counseling at the United Nations International School, NYC.

# ALSO BY JANE S. GABIN

*The Paris Photo: A Novel* (Wisdom House, Chapel Hill, 2018)

*American Women in Gilded Age London: Expatriates Rediscovered* (University Press of Florida, 2006)

Introduction to a new edition of Elizabeth L. Banks's 1928 autobiography, *The Remaking of an American* (University Press of Florida, 2000)